In the Trenches

World War I

Sean Stewart Price

Steck Vaughn™

A Harcourt Achieve Imprint

www.Steck-Vaughn.com
1-800-531-5015

In the Trenches: World War I
By Sean Stewart Price

Cover ©Topham/The Image Works; p.5 ©Bettmann/CORBIS;
p.6 ©Bettman/CORBIS; p.9 ©Swim Ink 2, LLC/CORBIS; p.11 ©Swim
Ink 2, LLC/CORBIS; p.12 ©Bettman/CORBIS; p.15 ©The Granger
Collection, New York; p.18 ©Hulton-Deutsch Collection/CORBIS;
p.21 ©CORBIS; p.23 ©Hulton-Deutsch Collection/CORBIS;
p.24–25 ©CORBIS; p.29 ©Bettman/CORBIS.

Additional photography by Photos.com Royalty Free.

ISBN-13: 978-1-4190-2311-8
ISBN-10:   1-4190-2311-X

Printed in China

2 3 4 5 6 7 8 788 13 12 11 10 09

Table of Contents

Total War

On June 28, 1914, crowds lined the streets to see the Archduke Franz Ferdinand and his wife, Sophia. The place was Sarajevo (sair-uh-YAY-vo) in Bosnia. At that time, Bosnia belonged to the empire of Austria-Hungary. Archduke Franz Ferdinand was heir to the throne. He was warned to stay away. The Serbs who lived in Bosnia wanted to be free. Ferdinand's life would be in danger there. He didn't listen.

The royal couple rode in an open car. It moved slowly down the street. They greeted the public. Suddenly, a grenade exploded. Ferdinand and his wife were unhurt, but their guards were wounded. The couple tried to flee. A 19-year-old student stepped forward. He belonged to the Black Hands, a Serbian terrorist group. He shot the archduke and his wife. That was called the "shot heard round the world." Why? It began the "war to end all wars," also known as World War I.

After the archduke was **assassinated**, Austria-Hungary declared war on Serbia. Germany and the Ottoman Empire (now Turkey) joined the war, too. They had an **alliance** with Austria-Hungary. These countries were called the Central Powers.

The Serbs had protection from Russia. Russia had the support of France and Great Britain. These countries became known as the Allies.

This war would be different from any war that came before. At the end of the 1800s there had been a giant leap forward in technology. Fighter planes, machine guns, and poison gas were deadly new weapons. Battlefields were not places of honor. Soldiers hid in cold, stinking **trenches**. These holes often became their graves.

Why would the whole world go to war over an assassination? There were lots of reasons. European countries were expanding. They argued over land and power at home and abroad. Germany wanted colonies like the ones that Great Britain and France had in Africa. France and Germany both claimed the land along their border. The Balkan states were claimed by both Russia and Austria-Hungary. In addition, Austria-Hungary and the Ottoman Empire were being challenged by nations seeking independence. All this added up to the biggest grudge match the world had ever known.

By 1917, almost all of Europe was at war.

For a time, the United States remained **neutral**. The United States had a tradition of **isolationism**. American leaders tried to stay out of European conflicts.

This war, however, was hard to avoid. Both England and Germany tried to starve each other. They set up naval **blockades**. The Germans used submarines called U-boats. The U-boats attacked ships bringing supplies to Great Britain. Some German U-boats sank ocean liners carrying Americans.

In 1915, a U-boat attack brought the United States close to war. A German sub sank the British ocean liner *Lusitania*. The attack killed more than 120 Americans. In the United States, many people considered it an act of war.

Germany's king, Kaiser Wilhelm II, didn't want American troops in the war. He backed off. He ordered his U-boats to leave passenger liners alone.

The New York Times.

EXTRA
5:30 A.M.

"All the News That's Fit to Print."

ONE CENT

NEW YORK, SATURDAY, MAY 8, 1915.—TWENTY-FOUR PAGES.

VOL. LXIV. NO. 20928.

LUSITANIA SUNK BY A SUBMARINE, PROBABLY 1,260 DEAD;
TWICE TORPEDOED OFF IRISH COAST; SINKS IN 15 MINUTES;
CAPT. TURNER SAVED, FROHMAN AND VANDERBILT MISSING;
WASHINGTON BELIEVES THAT A GRAVE CRISIS IS AT HAND

SHOCKS THE PRESIDENT

Washington Deeply Stirred by the Loss of American Lives.

BULLETINS AT WHITE HOUSE

Wilson Reads Them Closely, but Is Silent on the Nation's Course.

HINTS OF CONGRESS CALL

Loss of Lusitania Recalls Firm Tone of Our First Warning to Germany.

CAPITAL FULL OF RUMORS

SOME DEAD TAKEN ASHORE

Several Hundred Survivors at Queenstown and Kinsale.

NOTICE

TRAVELLERS intending to embark on the Atlantic voyage are reminded that a state of war exists between Germany and her allies and Great Britain and her allies; that the zone of war includes the waters adjacent to the British Isles; that, in accordance with formal notice given by the Imperial German Government, vessels flying the flag of Great Britain, or of any of her allies, are liable to destruction in those waters and that travellers sailing in the war zone on ships of Great Britain or her allies do so at their own risk.

IMPERIAL GERMAN EMBASSY

The Lost Cunard Steamship Lusitania

Saw the Submarine 100 Yards Off and Watched Torpedo as it

Cunard Office Here Besieged for News; Fate of 1,918 on Lusitania Long in Doubt

List of Saved Includes Capt. Turner; Vanderbilt and Frohman Reported Lost

Spy Game

In Europe, the war turned into a stand-off. Neither side could gain ground. The two sides dug trenches across France to hold their ground. Millions of soldiers died.

Then, Room 40 made a discovery. Room 40 was the office where British **espionage** was based. They **intercepted** a lot of messages. Usually, the messages were dull. *A German ship had sailed. A general had won a promotion.*

Then, Room 40 spies uncovered a special telegram on January 17, 1917. It came from German diplomat Arthur Zimmermann. It looked like a sheet of long numbers. Slowly, the British experts translated the code. Words like "submarine," "Mexico," and "Japan" appeared. The code breakers knew they had something big.

The message offered Mexico a deal. If the United States joined the Allies, Germany would help Mexico invade the United States. At war's end, Mexico would get Texas, New Mexico, and Arizona. The Zimmermann Telegram hinted at a similar deal with Japan. It also said that U-boats would attack again.

The British shared the telegram with President Woodrow Wilson. It was enough to push Wilson over the edge. On April 6, 1917, Congress voted to join the Allies. The United States began to prepare for total war.

The *Lusitania* carried many American passengers when she departed from New York for Liverpool on May 1, 1915. The *Lusitania* was known for its speed, and it was thought to be safe against the attacks of enemies.

A Nation in Training

By 1917, President Wilson was ready for war. What about the rest of the country? The U.S. military needed lots of soldiers. Millions of young men left their jobs. Someone had to take their places. The soldiers needed uniforms, guns, tanks, and airplanes. Total war required total effort. "It is not an army we need to train and shape for war," said Wilson. "It is a nation."

Selling the War

In 1916, Wilson had won his second term as President. His slogan had been, "He kept us out of war." Just months after the election, Wilson changed his mind. He wanted Americans to go to war. How did he explain the shift? He warned that the Central Powers were ruled by dictators. This war would make the world "safe for democracy," he said. Many Americans didn't believe him. So Wilson launched the biggest ad campaign the nation had ever seen.

To lead the campaign, Wilson created the Committee for Public Information (CPI). Former journalist George Creel ran the CPI. His job was to create patriotic advertising, or **propaganda**. Creel wanted every home united in the war effort. He promised to "weld the American people into one white hot mass."

The CPI spent millions of dollars to do it. Filmmakers produced pro-war movies. Authors wrote patriotic books and magazine articles. Artists made colorful posters. The most famous was James Montgomery Flagg's army **recruiting** poster. It showed Uncle Sam pointing toward the reader and saying "I Want You." Creel also used live presentations. He hired 75,000 "Four-Minute" men and women. These speakers made brief speeches at movie theaters and public meetings.

The CPI often used fear to reach its audience. "Four-Minute" speakers told people to watch out for **traitors**. Posters accused German troops of killing civilians.

TEAMWORK BUILDS SHIPS

UNITED STATES SHIPPING BOARD ISSUED BY PUBLICATIONS SECTION EMERGENCY FLEET CORPORATION PHILADELPHIA PA EMERGENCY FLEET CORPORATION

Many ad campaigns like this one encouraged people to support the war.

Creel's committee also **censored** other publications. Articles and photos that might hurt the war effort could not be published. Soon, everything German seemed **suspicious**. Many people decided to change their German-sounding names. Some places even banned German products, like hot dogs or Beethoven recordings. One sign in Chicago read, "Danger to pro-Germans! Loyal Americans Welcome to Edison Park."

The CPI helped Wilson get his message across. In January 1918, Wilson laid out his "Fourteen Points." They were Wilson's plan for the world after the war ended. Wilson promised to rebuild invaded countries. He wanted to support democracy. He wanted to create the League of Nations to settle conflicts peacefully.

Creel's work paid off. Before long, most Americans supported the war effort. They bought more than $20 billion in war bonds. The bonds were a way of loaning money to the government to help pay for the war. Americans also planted "Victory Gardens" to raise their own food. People used less fuel so there would be more for the troops. People everywhere sang George M. Cohan's hit song, "Over There." *Over There, Over There / Send the word, send the word, / Over There / That the Yanks are coming, / The Yanks are coming, / The drums rum tumming everywhere.*

I WANT YOU
FOR U.S. ARMY
NEAREST RECRUITING STATION

The U.S. military needed nearly five million men by the end of the war. The government printed 4 million copies of this recruiting poster. It became one of the best-known images in the country.

The Army Wants You

Americans were ready for war. Yet, the U.S. military was in no shape to fight. The army had only 127,500 men in April 1917. By war's end, it would need more than four million. Another 800,000 served in the navy and other military branches.

Finding, supplying, and training all those people was a huge task. A steady line of volunteers showed up. It wasn't enough. So in May 1917, Congress passed a military **draft**. It was the first draft since the Civil War ended in 1865. One U.S. senator thought it would lead to riots. It didn't. Creel's propaganda helped ease objections. The draft brought in seven out of every ten soldiers.

Sending men off to war created a labor shortage. For the first time, women worked factory jobs.

Women at Work

From coast to coast, men left their jobs to join the military. Millions of women took over their jobs. They worked in factories making guns, bombs, and planes. They drove trucks. They helped run railroads. They repaired machines. Many of these women had never worked outside the home before. Most of them had never voted, either. At the time, only ten states allowed women to vote.

Women even served near the front lines. Many worked in France for the YMCA and the Salvation Army. They cooked, cleaned, and cared for the troops. About 21,000 women served in the Army Nurse Corps. Some 12,000 more worked for the navy and marines. They handled communications and paperwork. That freed men to fight on the front lines.

For many young men, joining the military seemed the only patriotic choice. Most hated the strict military rules. Yet, civilians often treated new soldiers like celebrities. Corporal Frederick Pottle enjoyed a trip from one base to another. "The Red Cross women met us at the stations, showering us with gifts," he said. "Whistles blew, and everyone shouted and waved flags."

At camp, the soldiers trained for three months. Then, they boarded ships and headed "Over There" to war.

Fighting for
RESPECT

The United States fought for democracy overseas. Yet, its own military didn't live up to this goal. About 200,000 African Americans served in Europe during the war. They served in **segregated** units. Only 42,000 black soldiers were allowed to fight. The rest did the hardest and dirtiest work. In other branches of the military, they didn't even get that far. The navy and marines barred African Americans from most kinds of service.

Still, the war brought pride to many African Americans. Four black units helped the French army. The French had no history of racism. They treated the black Americans like any other soldiers.

New York's 369th Infantry became the most famous African-American unit. Their bravery won them the nickname "Harlem Hellfighters." They earned more than 170 French medals during the war.

At the war's end, black soldiers came home to a lot of changes. Many blacks who stayed home had done well. The war effort had created thousands of jobs. Before the war, African American women often worked cleaning homes. During the war, they got jobs in factories and businesses. "I'll never work in nobody's kitchen but my own no more," said one new factory worker.

Harlem staged a grand parade for the Hellfighters. The unit's captain, Arthur Little, described the scene. "Mothers, and wives, and sisters, and sweethearts rushed right out through the ranks to embrace [us].... Every fourth soldier had a girl upon his arm—and we marched through Harlem singing and laughing."

At least for the moment, Captain Little felt as though race didn't matter. "On February 17, 1919," he wrote, "New York City knew no color line."

Some American generals thought black soldiers wouldn't fight with courage. Units like the Harlem Hellfighters proved the generals wrong.

Over There

The first U.S. troops arrived in Europe in June 1917. Cheering crowds greeted them in Paris, France. General John J. Pershing commanded the American Expeditionary Force (AEF). He marched the U.S. troops to the tomb of the Marquis de Lafayette. Lafayette had helped Americans win the Revolutionary War. "Lafayette, we are here!" declared one of Pershing's officers.

The French and British were happy to see fresh troops. European troops were exhausted. They had been fighting on the Western Front for three years. The Western Front was a long system of trenches that extended 708 kilometers (440 miles). It ran across northern France. Huge battles raged there. Hundreds of thousands of soldiers died on the front. And what for? In two and a half years, the line had barely moved. It rarely shifted more than ten miles in either direction. And soldiers died there every day.

Vera Brittain served near the front. She was a young English nurse. Brittain treated soldiers who had been wounded in the trenches. The British Army was full of "tired, nerve-wracked men," she said. Next to them, the Americans looked optimistic and "so magnificent."

The Allies battled the Central Powers on many different fronts. Most American troops helped support the Allies along the Western Front. Russia defended the Eastern Front until October 1917. At that time, communist rebels overthrew the Russian government. Italy remained neutral until August 1916, when they joined the Allies. Fighting raged on the open seas, as well.

Soldiers lived under terrible conditions in the trenches. Rats and lice added to the misery of the war.

American soldiers saw their first combat in October 1917. They soon discovered what the Europeans already knew. New weapons had completely changed the nature of war. Combat was more deadly than ever. World War I soldiers faced the first tanks. Planes launched the first air raids on cities. Flamethrowers were widely used for the first time. Poison gas was shot into trenches. It burned out the lungs of unprepared soldiers.

One of the biggest changes was the machine gun. In the 1800s, rifles weren't very accurate. They took a long time to reload. Men marched at each other in the open. There was a lot of hand-to-hand combat. Now, the machine gun reduced the chances of survival.

The generals had learned their tactics many years earlier. They still sent men charging out of the trenches. Many attacks turned into **massacres**. A single machine gun could wipe out many soldiers at once. The area between the trenches was called "No Man's Land." Few survived enemy fire there for long.

Artillery shells killed more soldiers than any other weapon. Artillery guns had replaced old-fashioned cannons. They shot farther, and they could be rapidly reloaded. The shells exploded when they landed. A bombing from these large guns was terrifying.

One officer remembered it this way: "There is a faraway moan that grows to a scream, then a roar like a train…. A hunching of the shoulders and then another comes, and the thought—How long, how long? There is nothing to do. Whether you get through or not is just sheer chance and nothing more."

Life in the trenches was miserable. Enemy fire made it too dangerous to properly bury the dead. Rotting bodies everywhere attracted flies and rats. Rain turned the trenches into rivers of mud. Lice, or "cooties," also harassed soldiers. These tiny blood-sucking insects got into clothes and hair. They caused constant itching.

The stress was unbearable. Some soldiers suffered from "shell shock." It paralyzed them briefly. Others could not speak. Some developed twitches. Today, that condition is called "post-traumatic stress disorder."

Turning It Around

The big test for the Allies came in March 1918. A revolution in Russia had put **communist** rebels in power. The new Soviet government pulled out of the war. Thousands of German soldiers left the Eastern Front and moved to the Western Front. They launched new attacks on France from the trenches.

The Allied lines in France weakened under the assault. Fresh American troops plugged holes in the line. They helped boost Allied **morale**. Food and other supplies poured in from the United States. Exhausted French and British troops kept fighting. In June, they stopped the German advance.

In August 1918, the Allies launched a massive counterattack. General Pershing threw 1.2 million Americans into battle. The Allied troops just kept coming. The Germans saw no help in sight. Great Britain's naval blockade was working. Food, medicine, and fuel were hard to find in Germany. German troops started to leave the army in large numbers.

By October, both sides knew the end was near. Germany and the Central Powers were out of resources. The two sides agreed to stop fighting. They signed an **armistice** at 5:10 A.M. on November 11, 1918. Sadly, the cease-fire did not begin until 11 A.M. that morning. Allied officials wanted the war to end on the 11th hour of the 11th day of the 11th month. So the dying went on for six more hours.

Finally, the gunfire stopped. Silence fell over No Man's Land. "It was crazy," wrote one U.S. soldier. "At five minutes to eleven, we were trying to kill [the Germans], and they were doing the same to us. Yet, the magic hour came, and we found ourselves laughing and shaking hands with them."

The fighting stopped at 11 A.M. on November 11, 1918. It might have ended on November 8, when the peace talks began. This would have saved at least 6,600 lives.

"Well, It's Over"

Shirley Millard was an American nurse. She served at a French army hospital near the front lines. She was working there when the war ended. These entries are from her diary.

November 8, 1918 More and more Americans in the death ward. Gas cases are terrible. They cannot breathe lying down or sitting up. They just struggle for breath, but nothing can be done. Their lungs are gone. [Many are] covered with first-degree burns.

November 10 Charley [an injured soldier] died this morning. I held his hand as he went and could not keep back the tears. Near the end, he saw me crying and patted my hand to comfort me. I cannot describe that boy's sweetness. He took part of my heart with him.

Just after he went, someone came into the ward and said, "Armistice! The staff cars have just passed by the gate on their way … to sign the armistice!"

There is no armistice for Charley or for any of the others in that ward. One of the boys began to sob. I went and talked soothingly to him, but what could I say, knowing he would die before night?

Well, it's over. I have to keep telling myself, it's over.

But there is still that letter to write to Charley's mother. I can hear noise and shouting through the hospital as I write this. The chapel bell is ringing wildly.

I am glad it is over, but my heart is heavy as lead. Must write that letter.

One of the girls came looking for me. They have opened champagne for the staff in the dining hall. I told her to get out.

Can't seem to pull myself together.

At hospitals like this one, doctors and nurses worked around the clock during periods of heavy fighting. This nurse wears a mask to protect her from poison gas.

Safe for Democracy?

In the winter, American troops came home. The first shiploads arrived in New York. Huge flag-waving parades greeted them. "I felt a thrill," remembered one soldier. "I stopped and picked up a handful of dirt. It had been trampled by millions of feet, but it was part of our

These troops returning home are greeted with celebrations in New York City.

country. Someone asked me what I was doing. I said I was just shaking hands with America."

The reunion wasn't always easy. Many soldiers had trouble adjusting to life at home. The military gave each one a uniform, a coat, a pair of shoes, and $60. They were on their own. About four million young men were suddenly looking for work. Jobs were hard to find.

Wounded veterans struggled the most. Arthur Jensen came home with his brother. "It was hard for me and Walt," said Arthur. "We were both partially deaf from exploding shells. My throat was damaged by gas. Walt had a breaking out on his face from cootie bites." The physical wounds were just part of the damage, though. Arthur had seen too much on the battlefield. He found it hard to care about life at home.

People had died in staggering numbers. About 1.5 million Americans saw combat. More than 53,000 of them died in action. Another 63,000 died from disease or other causes. That was nothing compared to European losses. About 1.4 million French soldiers died. The Germans lost 1.8 million. In all, the war took nearly nine million military lives. Another six million civilians died.

The Great War helped start another tragedy, too. Each country kept its soldiers in cramped conditions. Spanish flu spread easily. Between 1917 and 1919, this killer disease spread around the world. It killed more than twenty million people. That's more lives than the fighting itself claimed.

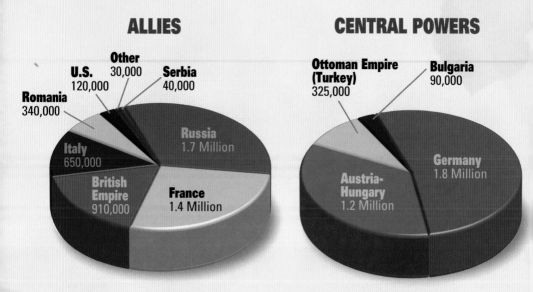

ALLIES

Other 30,000
U.S. 120,000
Serbia 40,000
Romania 340,000
Russia 1.7 Million
Italy 650,000
British Empire 910,000
France 1.4 Million

CENTRAL POWERS

Ottoman Empire (Turkey) 325,000
Bulgaria 90,000
Germany 1.8 Million
Austria-Hungary 1.2 Million

World War I was the most destructive war in history at the time. These pie charts show the number of deaths in the war.

A Lasting Peace?

After the fighting stopped, the Allied leaders met in Paris. Europe was a wreck. The war had killed millions of young men. It had destroyed railroads and farmland. Now, it was time to rebuild. But how? Where would the money come from? And how could the world avoid another terrible war?

President Wilson arrived in Paris with a plan. His **objective** was to "make the world safe for democracy." First, he wanted to rebuild the countries of the defeated Central Powers. He argued that strong economies would help create stable democracies. He also wanted to create a League of Nations. The League would be a world union. Its members would work together to keep the peace.

The Great War officially ended when the Treaty of Versailles was signed on June 28, 1919, in Paris. The treaty supported Wilson's League of Nations. Yet, France and Great Britain rejected the rest of Wilson's plan. Both nations were still angry over the war. They wanted to keep the Central Powers weak. The French were especially bitter. The fighting had destroyed many French towns and farms. French leaders wanted Germany to pay for all the losses.

Germany did pay heavily. The country lost around 13 percent of its land. About 9 percent of its population had lived there. It also paid billions of dollars to the Allies. Plus, France and Great Britain **seized** German colonies in Africa.

Wilson went home worried. His hopes for lasting peace rested with the League of Nations. Yet, Americans were suspicious. Many people felt the League would take power away from the United States.

The President toured the country. He pleaded with Americans to support the League. Without it, he said, "there will be another world war."

Wilson pushed hard. He planned to make 35 speeches in three weeks. During the trip, though, he suffered a massive stroke. He was forced to return to Washington and rest.

In the end, the U.S. Senate voted against the League of Nations. Without the support of the United States, the League had little power. Wilson died in 1924. His dreams of a lasting peace were shattered.

By the late 1920s, many people felt the war had been a waste. Millions had died. The world was sinking into an economic **depression**. Dictators were coming to power in Europe. World War I had been called the "war to end all wars." Instead, it had caused more destruction than any war in history.

In Germany, things were changing for the worse. After the war, Germans were furious. Many refused to admit defeat. "You didn't lick us," one German soldier told an American. "We knew when to quit. We'll be back in twenty years."

The soldier was right. During World War I, Adolf Hitler was a soldier in the German army. After the war, he became a politician. Hitler used German anger over the treaty to gain power. He blamed Germany's surrender on wealthy Jews. Ordinary soldiers had been "stabbed in the back," he claimed.

In 1933, Hitler's Nazi Party took power in Germany. Hitler quickly became a dictator. Six years later, he invaded Poland. World War II had begun. By the time it ended, fifty million more people were dead.

President Woodrow Wilson was awarded the 1920 Nobel Peace Prize. However, he was unable to gain support in the United States for the League of Nations.

Glossary

alliance (*noun*) an agreement between two countries or groups to work together

armistice (*noun*) a temporary agreement to stop fighting

artillery (*noun*) large guns with a long range

assassinate (*verb*) to murder by a sudden and secret attack, usually for political reasons

blockade (*noun*) an organized effort to close off an area so no supplies get through

censor (*verb*) to remove part of a publication or movie because it might be offensive or harmful

communist (*adjective*) having to do with a government in which the state controls the economy

depression (*noun*) a time when businesses and the economy do poorly

draft (*noun*) required duty to serve in the military

espionage (*noun*) the use of spying to get information

intercept (*verb*) to stop something from getting where it's going

isolationism (*noun*) a government policy of avoiding alliances or conflicts with other countries

massacre (*noun*) a large-scale killing

morale (*noun*) the spirit or level of confidence of a person or group

neutral (*adjective*) not supporting any group in a conflict or disagreement

objective (*noun*) a goal

propaganda (*noun*) information designed to influence the way people think

recruiting (*adjective*) trying to sign someone up for military service

segregated (*adjective*) kept separate from the main group, often because of race

seize (*verb*) to take possession of something

suspicious (*adjective*) tending to believe that something is wrong

traitor (*noun*) someone who betrays his or her country

trench (*noun*) a long, narrow ditch used by soldiers for protection

Idioms

heart is heavy (page 23) to be sad
My heart was heavy when summer vacation ended.

Index